The Tallest Buildings

Susan K. Mitchell
AR B.L.: 5.6
Points: 1.0   MG

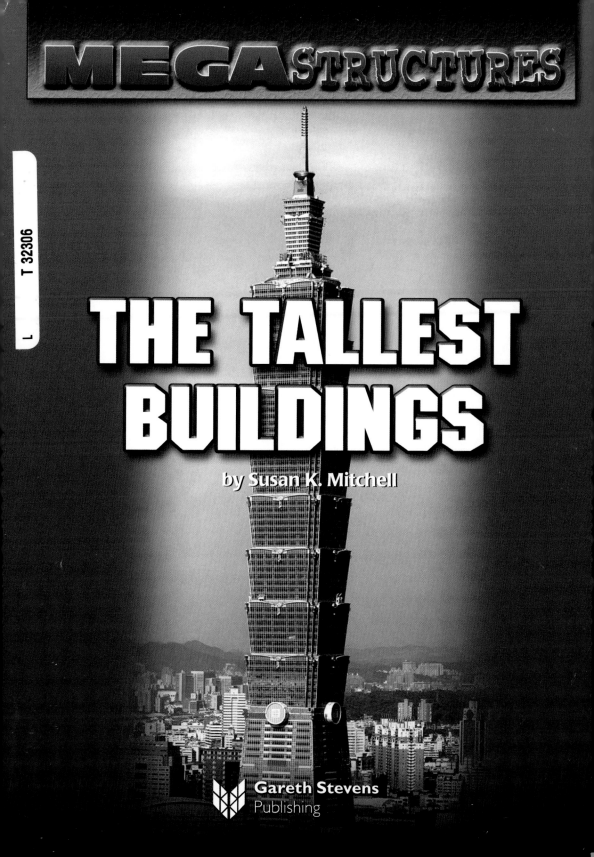

MEGASTRUCTURES

THE TALLEST BUILDINGS

by Susan K. Mitchell

Gareth Stevens
Publishing

Please visit our web site at: www.garethstevens.com
For a free color catalog describing Gareth Stevens Publishing's
list of high-quality books, call 1-800-542-2595 (USA)
or 1-800-387-3178 (Canada).

Library of Congress Cataloging-in-Publication Data

Mitchell, Susan K.
      The tallest buildings / by Susan K. Mitchell.
         p. cm. — (Megastructures)
      Includes bibliographical references and index.
      ISBN-13: 978-0-8368-8366-4 (lib. bdg.)
      ISBN-10: 0-8368-8366-7 (lib. bdg.)
      1. Tall buildings.   I. Title.
   NA6230.M58   2007
   720'.483—dc22   2007006979

This edition first published in 2008 by
Gareth Stevens Publishing
A Weekly Reader® Company
1 Reader's Digest Road
Pleasantville, NY 10570-7000 USA

Copyright © 2008 by Gareth Stevens, Inc.

Editorial direction: Mark J. Sachner
Editor: Barbara Kiely Miller
Art direction and design: Tammy West
Picture research: Diane Laska-Swanke
Production: Jessica Yanke
Illustrations: Spectrum Creative Inc.

Picture credits: Cover, title, pp. 16, 17, 24, 27 © AP Images;
pp. 5, 6 © Bettmann/CORBIS; p. 10 The Everett Collection;
p. 12 © CORBIS; pp. 14, 29 © Tim Sloan/AFP/Getty Images;
p. 19 © Jose Fuste Raga/CORBIS; p. 26 © Jon Hicks/CORBIS

Printed in the United States of America

1 2 3 4 5 6 7 8 9 11 10 09 08 07

CONTENTS

On the Cover: The Taipei 101 in Taiwan towers over the city streets as today's temporary title holder of the World's Tallest Building.

CHAPTER 1

A RACE TO THE SKY

In the 1950s, architect Frank Lloyd Wright designed an amazing building that would be taller than anything ever built. He called it The Illinois. The building would stand more than 5,000 feet (1,500 meters) high — that's nearly 1 mile (1.6 kilometers) tall. It sounded like science fiction, but Mr. Wright believed it could be built.

The Illinois never became more than a sketch. No building that tall has ever been built. Today, however, skyscrapers are getting closer to Wright's dream. New materials and ways of building are making super-tall skyscrapers possible. They are being built sky-high for many different reasons.

The Birth of Skyscrapers

Some buildings are built as important symbols of a city or country. People also build skyscrapers for other reasons. In some big cities, there is not enough land for all the people living and working there. By building upward, people can create more useable space on less land.

The first country to build skyscrapers was the United States. In the late 1800s, the country was growing. Land in some cities became harder to find and cost more to buy. Builders began to design tall buildings with many floors. But the only building materials at that time were stone or brick. Their weight limited how tall a building could be. The tallest buildings were only seven or eight stories high. Builders needed something else to make taller buildings. They needed a material to help support the weight of the stone and brick.

Steel was the answer. Steel is very flexible and strong, and people had been making it from iron for many years. In 1884, architect William LeBaron Jenney had the idea to use steel as a frame for buildings. The steel frame would work like a skeleton. It would hold up and support the weight

Going Up?

In the early 1800s, elevators were powered by steam engines. The engine ran a system of gears that turned a drum. A rope was attached to the drum. As the drum turned, the rope wound around the drum and pulled the elevator up. If the lifting rope broke, there was no way to stop the elevator from crashing to the ground. Elevators were not safe enough to carry people.

Elisha Graves Otis invented a safety brake for elevators. In 1853, he showed off his new brake at the World's Fair in New York. Standing on a raised elevator platform, Otis cut the elevator rope. The elevator began to fall with Otis still inside. Instead of crashing, the safety brake stopped the elevator in seconds. Otis' invention made elevators safe for people to use. It also meant buildings could be built higher than before.

of the building. Jenney built the Home Insurance Building in Chicago, Illinois. It was the very first steel frame skyscraper.

Fighting for the Title

Since that first skyscraper, new building materials and methods have been found. They have made it possible to build skyscrapers more than ten times higher than those early buildings.

Three years after unveiling his elevator brake at the World's Fair (*shown here*), Otis designed the first passenger elevator in the United States.

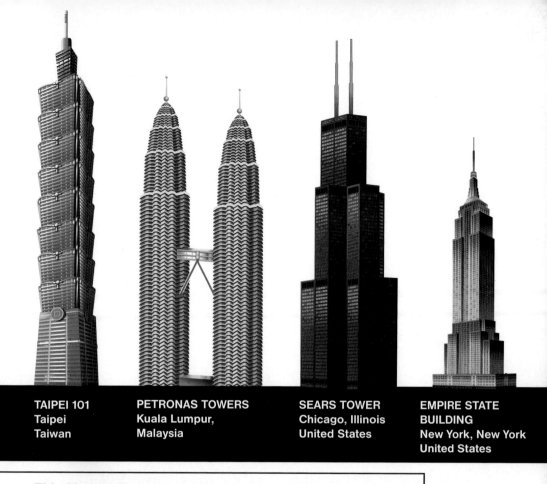

| TAIPEI 101 Taipei Taiwan | PETRONAS TOWERS Kuala Lumpur, Malaysia | SEARS TOWER Chicago, Illinois United States | EMPIRE STATE BUILDING New York, New York United States |

This illustration shows four of the world's current and past tallest buildings side by side.

But the tallest building today may not hold its title for long. Architects and builders are always working on bigger and better skyscrapers. One day, Frank Lloyd Wright's dream of a mile-high building may come true.

MEGA FACTS

The Burj Dubai skyscraper is now being built in the United Arab Emirates. When finished in 2008, it will become the new "World's Tallest Building."

7

CHAPTER 2

A NEW YORK GIANT

In the early 1900s, skyscrapers were going up all over New York City. Several builders competed to build the tallest skyscraper. In 1930, the Chrysler Building was the first building to exceed a height of 1,000 feet (305 m). It was a huge accomplishment for the Chrysler Corporation.

Then two men decided to build something taller. Alfred E. Smith had been governor of New York. John J. Raskob had worked for General Motors, one of Chrysler's competitors. Both men were very rich. They wanted their building to beat the Chrysler Building and become the world's tallest. But neither man knew anything about building skyscrapers. They hired architect William F. Lamb.

At the beginning of the project, Mr. Lamb's designs were very plain. Then one day he held up a sharp pencil and had a great idea. "The clean soaring lines inspired him," his wife said, "and he modeled the building after it."

Building codes required tall buildings to use setbacks in their design. Buildings with setbacks got narrower as they got taller. This kept the buildings from blocking all the sunlight to the street below.

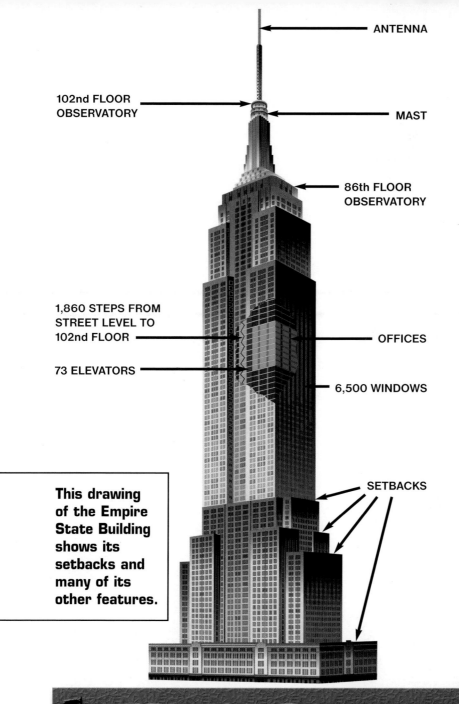

ANTENNA

102nd FLOOR
OBSERVATORY

MAST

86th FLOOR
OBSERVATORY

1,860 STEPS FROM
STREET LEVEL TO
102nd FLOOR

OFFICES

73 ELEVATORS

6,500 WINDOWS

SETBACKS

**This drawing
of the Empire
State Building
shows its
setbacks and
many of its
other features.**

MEGA FACTS

The top of the Empire State building was designed as a mast to dock **blimps**. These airships were filled with hydrogen. People traveled in them, much as they do in airplanes today.

Star of the Big Screen

The Empire State Building has appeared in more than sixty movies. *King Kong* is the most famous. It was first made in 1933, then remade in 1976 and 2005. In the first and third versions of the movie, Kong climbs up the Empire State Building and fights off airplanes. In the second version, he climbs up the World Trade Cener.

The Empire State Building also appears in *Independence Day*. In that movie, invading aliens blow up the building and all of New York City. In *Sky Captain and the World of Tomorrow*, the building is shown with a blimp docked at the mast on top of the skyscraper.

A small model of the Empire State Building was used to film this scene from *King Kong* in 1933.

Mr. Lamb designed the Empire State Building with a wide five-story base. Then several stories up, like stair steps, floors would be "set back" from the ones below.

An Economic Blow

Just as the plans for the Empire State Building were finished, the Great Depression began. The U.S. economy hit rock bottom. Banks and businesses closed. More than fifteen million people were out of work. Families struggled to find money for food and a place to live. Luckily, Mr. Raskob was very wealthy, and his fortune kept the Empire State Building project |going. It was able to provide jobs to workers hit hard by the Depression.

Construction began on March 17, 1930, and went amazingly fast. The steel workers and teams of riveters were able to finish one floor each day. Steel workers raised the steel beams and put them into place. Then the riveter teams took over. Every part of their job had to run like clockwork.

A worker called the "heater" heated the rivet over coals until it was red hot. Then he quickly tossed it to the "catcher." The catcher caught the burning hot

MEGA FACTS

The outside lights at the top of the Empire State Building change colors on holidays and during special events.

Defying Gravity

Some of the most dangerous jobs at the Empire State Building were done by Mohawk Indian steelworkers from Canada. They were called "skywalkers" because of their balance and lack of fear while working high in the sky. Their history began in 1886, when the Dominion Bridge Company hired several Mohawks to work on the Victoria Bridge in Canada. One bridge official said, "They would walk a narrow beam high up in the air with nothing below them. And it wouldn't mean any more to them than walking on the solid ground."

In the 1930s, the skyscraper boom brought many Mohawk workers and their families to New York. They helped build some of the tallest buildings in the United States. People on the street would often stop and look up to watch them work. Today, many Native Americans still work as skywalkers.

rivet in a can. He used tongs to put the rivet into a hole in the steel beam. Next, the "bucker-up" held the rivet in place for the "gunman," who fastened the rivet in place with a rivet gun.

Finally Finished

On May 1, 1931, the Empire State Building was finished. It took only one year and forty-five days to build it from start to finish. This time is still a record for a building this size. It has 102 floors and soars to a record-breaking height of 1,250 feet (381 m). For more than forty years, the Empire State Building was the "World's Tallest Building."

Working on the high, narrow beams of the Empire State Building was a dangerous job. Five workers died during the construction of the building.

CHAPTER 3

CHICAGO'S TURN

The Empire State Building may be famous, but it is not the tallest building in the world or even in the United States. In the United States, that title is held by the Sears Tower in Chicago, Illinois. In 1969, Sears was the largest store in the world. The bosses at Sears decided to move all their offices to one building in Chicago. With more than 350,000 workers all over the world, they were going to need a huge building.

Sears hired the architectural firm of Skidmore, Owings, and Merrill to plan the building. At first, the building was designed with only forty stories, but that number kept climbing higher. At one point, the design reached 104 stories. Eventually, six more floors were added to the design so the Sears Tower would become the World's Tallest Building. Workers began digging its foundation in August 1970.

Onward and Upward
The building's planners used a new building method to construct the Sears Tower. Called a bundled-tube design, this new method used several steel beams surrounded by a square tube of concrete. This design

used less steel than the traditional steel frame method. It also made buildings stronger and lighter than steel skeleton skyscrapers.

To reduce the effects of wind, the Sears Tower was designed to become narrower as it got taller. Its bottom fifty floors had nine steel and concrete tubes. These nine tubes used enough steel to build more than fifty thousand cars. For the next sixteen floors, only seven tubes kept going. The next twenty-three floors had four tubes. By the

MEGA FACTS

Six robotic window washing machines are mounted on the roof of the Sears Tower. They clean its 16,100 windows eight times each year.

ninety-first floor, only two tubes were left. Construction of the tubes began in June of 1971.

O, Christmas Tree

Large sections of steel for the Sears Tower were put together before being shipped to the building site. These sections, called "Christmas trees," were 25 feet (8 m) tall by 15 (5 m) feet wide. After they were put together, they were shipped to Chicago. Four cranes lifted the steel sections into place. The Christmas trees allowed work to get done very fast. Workers completed two floors each week. By March of 1972, the Sears Tower was half finished.

The building's designers wanted to try something new on the outside walls of the Sears Tower. Most skyscrapers had walls made of stone or brick. The Sears Tower designers needed a more modern look. They chose to use a silvery metal called aluminum. The only problem was that the

The Tallest or NOT the Tallest?

The Council on Tall Buildings and Urban Habitat (CTBUH) was formed in the 1970s. Its original job was to watch over part of the planning, design, and construction of tall buildings. But today the CTBUH is best known for keeping track of the World's Tallest Buildings list. In 1996, the CTBUH set up four categories for measuring the tallest building. They are the height to the top of an antenna, to the highest occupied floor, to the roof, and to the pinnacle, which is the long, pointed top of the building. Because of their giant pinnacles, the Petronas Towers in Malaysia were able to beat the Sears Tower as the "tallest." But the Sears Tower is still the tallest in three of the four CTBUH categories.

outside air would discolor the metal.

They fixed the problem by using an electric current to fuse a special coating to the metal. This gave the panels a black color and protected them from the weather. Workers finished the Sears Tower in 1973. Standing 1,454 feet (443 m) tall, it took its place as the new World's Tallest Building. The Sears Tower held onto the title until 1998.

This photo shows the top floor of the Sears Tower being built. The tall building in the distance on the left is the John Hancock Building.

MEGA FACTS

In August 1999, Alain "Spiderman" Robert climbed the outside of the Sears Tower. He did it without any safety gear. He used only his hands and feet to reach the top of the building.

The Sears Tower was struck by lightning during this 2003 storm. The building is hit by lightning between forty and ninety times each year.

Weird Weather

The height of super-tall buildings can bring some strange problems. The highest floors must be able to sway a few feet in strong winds. If the buildings did not move, they could snap in two. People who live and work on these top floors can become seasick as their buildings sway back and forth. Lightning can also strike super-tall skyscrapers. They have lightning rods, however, to prevent a direct strike. These buildings usually shield shorter buildings around them from being struck, too. Sometimes, winds blow so hard that rain and snow appear to be falling up instead of down. Birds may also crash into the top floors of a skyscraper during foggy weather.

17

CHAPTER 4

THE "OTHER" TWIN TOWERS

The United States is not the only country with super-tall buildings. As other countries have grown, so have their skyscrapers. Some were built to solve overcrowding problems. Others were built as a symbol of a country's wealth or power. The Petronas Towers of Kuala Lumpur, Malaysia, were built for this reason.

Malaysia is a small country in Southeast Asia. The country's prime minister wanted to build two huge buildings to show Kuala Lumpur's growing importance in the world. "When one is short, one should stand on a box to get a better view," he said. "The Petronas Twin Towers is to our ego what the box is to the shortie."

U.S. architect Cesar Pelli was hired to create the twin buildings. At first, being the tallest in the world was not talked about. The towers were originally designed to stand 1,380 feet (421m) tall. Then the Prime Minister saw the plans. He asked Pelli how

MEGA FACTS

The Petronas Towers hold more than just offices. A large concert hall, an art gallery, a shopping mall, and a science center can also be found inside.

Walking to the top of the Petronas Twin Towers is a long trip. Each tower has 765 flights of stairs.

much higher the buildings would have to be to capture the title of World's Tallest. When the men learned it would take only 75 feet (23 m) more, they decided to go for it.

Construction of the Petronas Towers began in 1993. Digging the towers' foundations was tricky.

The Original Twin Towers

The twin towers at the World Trade Center (WTC) in New York City were once the second tallest buildings in the United States. Completed in 1972 and 1973, they were the first skyscrapers built without any stone or brick. Each tower had 110 stories. One tower was 6 feet (2 m) taller than the other.

On September 11, 2001, terrorists hijacked American airplanes. They flew one airplane into each of the towers. While the top floors were badly damaged, the structures were still standing after the crashes. Then the heat from the burning jet fuel grew more intense and spread out unevenly. This caused the steel frames to lose even more strength. In a domino effect, the weakened upper floors began to collapse onto the floors below. In less than two hours, both World Trade Center towers collapsed completely.

Cesar Pelli studied local religions while designing the Petronas Towers. The main religion in Malaysia is Islam. Pelli based the buildings on an Islamic eight-point star. The star looks like one square turned at an angle on top of another square. It is a symbol of harmony and balance.

Mr. Pelli said, "These [shapes] are much more important in Islamic countries than in the West, and are understood ... and appreciated by everyone in their society." He also got design ideas from Islamic mosques. Each tower has a prayer room for the Muslims who work in the buildings.

The solid layer of rock that would secure them was far below the ground. Large steel beams had to be driven more than 300 feet (91 m) down. The beams worked like nails to hold the foundations in place. Trucks poured concrete on top of the steel beams for two straight days. It was the largest single concrete pour in history.

For added strength, Mr. Pelli used a tube-in-a-tube design. Workers constructed a tube of steel and high-strength concrete at the center of each building. Then they surrounded the center tube with an outer tube of sixteen equally spaced columns. Concrete beams connected the columns.

Gateway to the Sky

During the design of the towers' outside walls, one concern was Malaysia's high temperatures. Any material used for the outer walls had to help keep the inside of the buildings from becoming too hot. Mr. Pelli chose stainless steel. The shiny metal would reflect light and heat away from

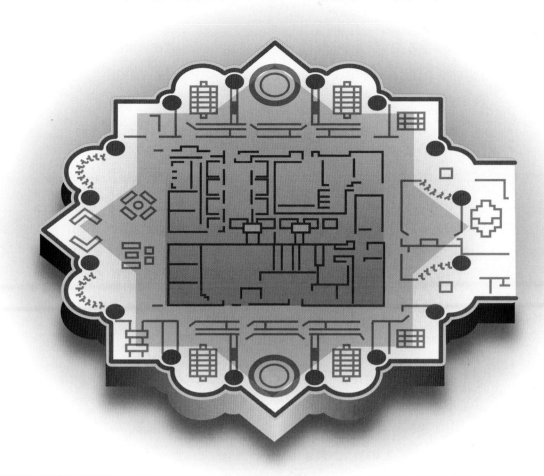

The shaded area on this diagram of a floor in the Petronas Twin Towers shows the shape of an Islamic star. In his design, building architect Cesar Pelli added half circles between each point.

the building. Also, depending on the sunlight and time of day, the metal would make the building look as if it were changing colors. Mr. Pelli had windows made of

MEGA FACTS

When empty, each tower weighs more than 330,000 tons (300,000 tonnes) — more than 50,000 elephants!

safety glass placed between the stainless steel panels.

The last challenge was building a skybridge between the towers. The bridge was built and tested in South Korea. When it was finished, it was shipped to Kuala Lumpur in more than four hundred pieces. The double-deck bridge weighed more than 700 tons (635 tonnes). It was 192 feet (59 m) long.

Crews spent an entire year practicing lifting the skybridge with a special machine. They had to lift it safely between the forty-first and forty-second floors of the two buildings. The machine that lifted the skybridge stopped twice when lightning knocked out the power. More than three days were needed to finally lift the bridge into place. Then workers connected it to the two towers.

By early 1996, the Petronas Towers were finished. Including the pinnacles on top, each building was 1,483 feet (452 m) tall. The title of World's Tallest Building would not last long, however. Another skyscraper was already climbing higher.

MEGA FACTS

Building designers used computerized models to test the strength of the skybridge. They also tested a model of it in a wind tunnel. They had to make sure it would not snap in half in high winds.

CHAPTER 5

A TITAN FROM TAIPEI

I n October 2003, workers placed a giant pinnacle on top of the Taipei 101 building. With this crowning event, the Taipei 101 beat all other skyscrapers for the title of World's Tallest Building. Designed by architect C.Y. Lee, the Taipei 101 takes its name from its location in Taipei, which is the capital of the Asian nation of Taiwan. The number in the building's name boasts of its 101 floors above ground. The building also has five floors below ground.

Mr. Lee had some unusual things to think about when designing the Taipei 101. The architects of all skyscrapers have to think about wind. Mr. Lee, however, also had to consider earthquakes! Taiwan is in an area of the world known for huge earthquakes. Mr. Lee tackled the earthquake problem by using a Tuned Mass Damper, or TMD.

The TMD is a huge metal ball hanging in the middle of the building. It weighs 730 tons (662 tonnes) and works like a pendulum. When the building sways in one direction, the TMD swings to the other side. The massive weight of the TMD straightens the building.

The Taipei 101 was built to survive a powerful

earthquake. But some people believe that the building might be causing earthquakes instead. "The stress added by the towers' weight is like the straw that breaks the camel's back," said earthquake expert Cheng-Horng Lin. He said that since the skyscraper was built, the number of earthquakes in Taiwan has doubled. The quakes have also become stronger. Two earthquakes began directly under the

MEGA FACTS

People sometimes hold races in skyscrapers. Runners start at the ground floor. Then they race up the stairs to the top of the building.

Taipei 101. So far, no one has been able to prove if the building itself is the cause of the earthquakes.

The outside of the Taipei 101 reflects ancient traditions, but the inside is very high-tech. The elevators in the Taipei 101 are the fastest in the world. They race at a speed of 37 miles (60 kilometers) per hour. They can move people eighty-nine stories in less than forty seconds.

The Race Continues

At 1,671 feet (509 m), the Taipei 101 is currently the World's Tallest Building. But it may not be for long. Several buildings are being designed or built that will climb even higher in a few years. The Burj Dubai, a skyscraper being built in the Middle East, looks as if it will reach that goal first. It was designed by the same company that designed the Sears Tower.

How tall the Burj Dubai will be has been kept a secret. It is expected to be more than 2,600 feet (792 m). That height will

Ancient Chinese Secrets

C.Y. Lee wanted to use both Chinese traditions and modern technologies in his design. A feng shui expert was hired. Feng shui is the ancient practice of placing furniture, buildings, and other objects to create a good flow of energy. The expert helped design and plan the Taipei 101.

Mr. Lee also used different Chinese symbols in the building. The number eight is considered lucky by the Chinese. The Taipei 101 has eight upwardly slanted sections. Each section has eight floors. The building looks like a stalk of bamboo shooting toward the sky. Bamboo represents strength and flexibility to the Chinese.

Building Boom

Five of the ten tallest buildings in the world are in China. Four of them are taller than the Empire State Building. The city of Shanghai has twice as many skyscrapers as New York City. Many of these buildings have been designed by American companies.

The Jin Mao Building in Shanghai was designed by Skidmore, Owings, and Merrill. They also designed the Sears Tower. Two Financial Centre in Hong Kong was designed by Cesar Pelli, the architect of the Petronas Towers. The designs of both buildings also include the number eight. Many of the highest Chinese buildings have either eighty-eight or eighty floors.

Shanghi's Jin Mao Building (*right*) contains the world's highest hotel rooms. The Grand Hyatt Hotel occupies floors 53 through 87.

Traditional camel racers contrast with the modern design of the Burj Dubai (*center*). When the building is completed, its pinnacle will be seen from 60 miles (96 km) away.

make it the first building to be one half-mile tall. Frank Lloyd Wright's dream of putting up a mile-high building may never be realized. But the lure of building the World's Tallest Building will continue to keep architects and builders reaching for the sky!

MEGA FACTS

The outdoor observation deck of the Taipei 101 is the highest in the world. It is located on the ninety-first floor.

TIME LINE

1853 Elisha Graves Otis invents elevator safety brake.

1885 William LeBaron Jenney builds the Home Insurance Building in Chicago. It has the first steel skeleton frame ever built.

1929 The Great Depression begins.

1930 The Chrysler Building in New York City is finished.

1931 The Empire State Building in New York City is completed. It has 102 floors and stands 1,250 feet (381 m) tall.

1956 Frank Lloyd Wright designs a mile-high building called The Illinois.

1973 World Trade Center towers are built in New York City.

1974 Construction of the Sears Tower in Chicago, Illinois is finished. It has 110 floors and stands 1,454 feet (443 m) tall.

1996 The Petronas Towers in Kuala Lumpur, Malaysia are complete. They both have 88 floors and stand 1,483 feet (452 m) tall.

2001 The World Trade Center towers are destroyed in a terrorist attack.

2003 The Taipei 101 in Taiwan is finished, becoming the current World's Tallest Building. It has 101 floors and stands 1,671 feet (509 m).

2006 Construction begins on the Burj Dubai in the United Arab Emirates.

GLOSSARY

aluminum — a thin, light, silvery metal

architect — a person who designs buildings and other structures

blimps — large gas-filled airships once used for travel

building codes — sets of rules and regulations that control the design, construction, and use of buildings

concrete — a mixture of cement, sand, pebbles, and water. It dries hard like stone.

economy — a country's system of money and resources

floors — levels of a building

foundation — the base on which a building is built

fuse — to combine or blend two or more materials together to make one

Great Depression — a period of deep financial trouble in the United States. It began in October 1929 and lasted for most of the 1930s.

mosques — Muslim places of worship

pendulum — an object hung so that it swings back and forth

pinnacle — the long, thin, and pointed top of a building

prime minister — a person in charge of a country, like a president

rivet — a fastener that is similar to a bolt. It is used to hold two or more pieces of metal together.

riveters — workers who connect building materials with rivets

skybridge — a bridge connecting one building with another for people to walk through

stainless steel — a special type of steel that is resistant to rusting

symbols — objects that stand for something else and have particular meanings

TO FIND OUT MORE

Books

Skyscrapers. Susan E. Goodman (Alfred A. Knopf)

Skyscrapers! Super Structures to Design and Build.
  Carol A. Johman (Williamson Publishing)

The Empire State Building. Great Buildings (series).
  Gini Holland (Raintree Steck-Vaughn)

The Sears Tower. Building America (series). Craig A.
  and Katherine M. Doherty (Blackbirch Press)

The Tallest Building. Extreme Places (series). Janet
  Halfmann (Kidhaven Press)

Video

Super Structures of the World: Skyscrapers (Unipix Home
  Entertainment) NR

Web Sites

Skyscrapers
www.emporis.com
Use this index to look up skyscrapers all over the world.

The Skyscraper Museum
www.skyscraper.org
Find information about several tall buildings.

Search for Skyscrapers
www.greatbuildings.com
Search for specific buildings.

Publisher's note to educators and parents: Our editors have carefully reviewed these Web sites to ensure that they are suitable for children. Many Web sites change frequently, however, and we cannot guarantee that a site's future contents will continue to meet our high standards of quality and educational value. Be advised that children should be closely supervised whenever they access the Internet.

About the Author

Susan K. Mitchell lives near Houston, Texas, where there are many tall buildings. She is a teacher and the author of several picture books. Susan has also written many non-fiction chapter books for kids. She has a wonderful husband, two daughters, a dog, two cats, and an adopted pet squirrel. She dedicates this book to her nephews, Mitch and Chris.